HEALTHY
RAW FOOD
COOKBOOK

HEALTHY
RAW FOOD
COOKBOOK

Plant-Based Meals to Help You Feel Revitalized and Recharged

SUSANNE ROTH

Skyhorse Publishing

Skyhorse Publishing books may be purchased in bulk at special discounts for sales
promotion, corporate gifts, fund-raising, or educational purposes. Special editions
can also be created to specifications. For details, contact the Special Sales Department,
Skyhorse Publishing, 307 West 36th Street, 11th Floor, New York, NY 10018 or
info@skyhorsepublishing.com.

Skyhorse® and Skyhorse Publishing® are registered trademarks of Skyhorse Publishing,
Inc.®, a Delaware corporation.

Visit our website at www.skyhorsepublishing.com.

10 9 8 7 6 5 4 3 2 1

Library of Congress Cataloging-in-Publication Data is available on file.

Cover design by David Ter-Avanesyan
Cover photo credit: Shutterstock

Print ISBN: 978-1-5107-6487-3
Ebook ISBN: 978-1-5107-7015-7

Printed in China

CONTENTS

Kitchen Equipment

I often get asked what equipment I have in my raw food kitchen. The following are the items I find helpful and use quite often.

Knives: You can do almost anything you need to do with a good, sharp chopping knife and a paring knife. Your knives are important and worth investing in. Keep them sharp to avoid accidents.

Food Processor: I use a KitchenAid food processor. It is my favorite. It is important to note that different food processors have different-sized motors, which means it may take longer for those with smaller motors to get the job done.

Dehydrators: I use the TSM stainless steel dehydrator. Another favorite among raw foodists is the Excalibur. I have both. You want to make sure that your dehydrator has a temperature control.

Spiral Cutter: A good spiral cutter is a great asset for your kitchen. It makes vegetable noodles from all kinds of veggies, such as zucchini.

High-Speed Blenders: There are two high-speed blenders that are really worth mentioning. One is the Vitamix and the other is the Blendtec. I have both in my kitchen and they each work very well. The Vitamix relies on a plunger to work with more difficult food, while the Blendtec has a variable speed. The Vitamix is a little heavier and more expensive. It's easier to get your food out of the Blendtec, which has a wide jar.

Magic Bullet Blender: These powerful little blenders work great when you only need to blend a small amount. They are reasonably priced and, with the two different blades, are very versatile.

Microplane: Initially developed as a woodworking tool, this grater is amazing in the kitchen. You can get them in many different sizes. They quickly grate ginger and garlic or zest lemons and oranges.

Mandoline Slicer: A great way to slice fruits and veggies. You can slice from ¼ inch to paper thin. Check prices. They range from very expensive to inexpensive. Make sure you get one that is easy to slice with and use caution.

Whisk: I have whisks in many sizes in my kitchen. When I am mixing up a quick ganache, there is nothing better. The smaller ones work great when you have small amounts. Make sure you have a small whisk and a medium whisk for starters.

Sprouting Jars: I like to keep a couple of different sizes on hand. These are glass jars with mesh tops that screw on. They make sprouting very easy.

Springform Pans: Springform pans are wonderful when making cheesecakes and some tarts. They are metal pans that have removable bottoms, making unmolding very easy.

Tart Pans: I have a large collection of tart pans. These are pans that have fluted edges and removable bottoms. I love the smaller sizes for individual servings and the larger sizes when I want to make a larger tart. They are good for both sweet and savory dishes.

Baking Rings: Baking rings are metal rings that are about 3½ inches in diameter and about 3 inches tall. They are great when making stacked food.

Helpful Hints

Dehydration: In the raw food world, the dehydrator is your oven. It is a very versatile piece of equipment that allows you to make "baked" items without destroying the vitamins, minerals, enzymes, and other nutrients that occur naturally in our food.

The dehydrator works by circulating warm air around food. By keeping the temperature below 116°F, we keep the nutrients in the food intact. The dehydrator opens the door to gourmet raw food, allowing endless menu possibilities. Veggie chips, eggplant "bacon," burgers, breads, and crackers are just some of the treats you will discover.

The most important thing to remember with dehydration is that the food temperature needs to stay under 116°F. You will notice that many times (not every), I start dehydration at a higher temperature and then reduce the temperature after an hour. Many people question if this is still considered raw. Rest assured, it is. The food temperature is what we are concerned with here, and in that first hour, the food being dehydrated is only kicking off moisture. The food temperature never goes over 115°F. Just remember to turn the temperature down after the initial time period. Setting a kitchen timer is the easiest way to do this.

There are quite a few benefits from dehydrating this way. First, it cuts the dehydration time down quite a bit, using less energy, which is better for our planet. Second, it helps prevent bacteria growth and fermentation that can occur when you dehydrate at lower temperatures for longer periods of time.

It is a good idea to rotate your shelves when you are dehydrating. You can rotate them from front to back and from top to bottom. The back and the top of the dehydrators are the warmest places.

I also calibrate my dehydrators. An oven thermometer works well for this. Place it on the top shelf and let it run long enough to get an accurate temperature.

Times are estimates. Different dehydrators will dry at different speeds. Air humidity can even affect drying times. The best way to deal with this is to keep an eye on your food as it dehydrates.

There are certain foods that you are going to want to dehydrate completely dry, such as crackers and flatbreads. Others should be somewhat chewy. The recipes give you suggested times and textures.

Ingredients: Always make sure you are using the freshest ingredients when making your raw recipes. Fruit should be ripe, but not overly ripe. Vegetables should be fresh and used as close to purchasing as possible. We don't have the option of cooking to cover up not-so-great ingredients. So, do yourself a big favor and use the best possible ingredients that you can get.

Frozen Vegetables and Fruits: I often get asked about frozen vegetables and fruits. If you can't get fresh, frozen can work in a pinch. I opt for organic. Vegetables and fruits that are flash frozen on the spot, directly after picking, often have more nutrients than fresh produce that has been picked too early and shipped thousands of miles.

Storing Raw Food: I often get asked how long recipes keep. Honestly, just use common sense. If it is something that has been dehydrated completely dry (like flatbreads), it will last much longer than something that still has moisture in it. Everything else? It's raw, fresh food. Treat it as such.

Storage Containers: With all the information on plastics leaching chemicals into our foods, I prefer to use glass containers to store food. They work great in the refrigerator and freezer. They do have plastic tops, but if your food isn't touching, you should be OK.

Make Sprouting Grains and Seeds

Sprouting Grains and Seeds: Sprouted grains and seeds are super-nutrition-packed powerhouse jewels. When you sprout grains, their life force is activated. You are literally taking a dry grain and turning it into a living, growing plant. When the growth cycle is activated, all kinds of wonderful things happen. Vitamin C and Vitamin B increase. Carotene increases while phytic acid (a substance we don't want) gets neutralized. Sprouting concentrates the nutrients and also makes the grains easier to digest. And even the enzymes that we love so much are increased during sprouting.

Sprouting Is Easy: Put a cup or two (what ever the recipe calls for) of the grain into a jar, fill the jar with water, and let it soak overnight. In the morning, pour off the water and rinse two to three times a day until you see a little tail starting to grow. At this point, you can dehydrate the grains and grind them into sprouted flour or use them as is.

Sprouted seeds can be added to salads, wraps, and many other dishes for taste, nutrients, and a little added crunch.

Substitutions: There isn't a day that goes by that I don't get a request for substitutions. People seem to have issues with nuts, flax, avocado, young Thai coconut, and grains. Substitution requests are frustrating because it isn't as simple as one would think.

When I create a recipe, great care is taken when combining ingredients. I am looking for a balance between the flavors, textures, and of course, visual appeal. How the ingredients interact with each other is also very important. Changing one ingredient can affect how the recipe comes together.

Balance is very important because without it, your food won't be appealing. That said, feel free to experiment. Taste as you go and be aware of the role the ingredient that you are replacing plays. If it is the backbone of the recipe, be cautious. But when substituting things that are very similar (for example, raisins for Craisins), go for it and have fun!

Buying Seasonally: It is always a good idea to try to make recipes with ingredients that are in season. You will save money and also get the freshest produce available. You can also freeze many fruits and veggies. Just know that the texture may change. Example: I freeze a lot of zucchini, but only in pureed form.

Maple Syrup: It is not raw, but is frequently used in raw food recipes.

Soaking Nuts

You will notice that many of the recipes in this book call for nuts and seeds to be soaked overnight. There are two reasons for this. First, nuts and seeds contain enzyme inhibitors that make them harder to digest. When soaked overnight, these enzyme inhibitors are deactivated, allowing for easier digestion. Second, many of the recipes call for nuts to be soaked for textural reasons. Cashews will blend more smoothly when presoaked, for example.

Some nuts, like cashews, are soaked for texture and for the moisture this brings to a recipe. Other nuts, such as almonds and walnuts, should be presoaked to release enzyme inhibitors. I always soak nuts for 8 hours when I first get them; then I dehydrate them until dry. That way I always have soaked nuts on hand for a recipe. If I need "wet" nuts for a recipe, I simply resoak them.

Dehydrating Fruit

Preparing the Fruit

Most fruits and berries may be dried satisfactorily. Select fresh, firm, ripe fruit. Discard all bruised or decayed fruits. (One piece of slightly spoiled fruit may flavor the entire lot.) Select late varieties in apples.

Thoroughly clean all products. Use stainless steel knives for cutting (carbon steel will discolor fruit). Slice everything ³⁄₁₆-inch thick; as you gain experience, you will find there are some items you may not want to slice, such as apricots, prunes, plums, cherries, etc. As apples, pears, peaches, etc., are peeled and cored or pitted, and sliced, prepare only enough fruit to fill one tray at a time. Dip in prepared solution of one tablespoon erythorbic acid or ascorbic acid dissolved in one gallon water. Soak fruit slices for two minutes only and drain thoroughly. Two minutes is entirely adequate and longer soaking will lengthen the drying time considerably.

When slices are the same thickness, the fruit will dry evenly. It is not necessary, however, to measure each slice. The slices should be placed close together, just touching, but only one layer deep so there is adequate air circulation. Immediately place the slices on nylon netting on the trays and put them into a dehydrator (or oven or out-of-doors). Remember, speed is very important in preparing fruit for drying by any method. You may then proceed to fill the other trays in the same manner until the dehydrator is filled. (Refer to Chart 1, Condensed Directions for Dehydration of Fruits.)

When dehydrating fruits such as apricots, plums, etc., the dehydrating time can be reduced by doing the following:

1. Break or cut the fruit in half and remove the pit.

2. Take one half in both hands, placing both thumbs in the middle of the skin side.

3. Turn the half "inside out." This breaks open the fibers, as you will see when this method is used, thereby reducing the drying time. With a little practice, this method is very easy and extremely effective. (We are indebted to Dora D. Flack for this idea.)

Different varieties of fruit can be dehydrated at the same time, placing a different variety on each shelf. However, do not mix fruits and vegetables in the same dehydrator load.

Special Treatment of Fruit Before Dehydrating

These suggestions should be used only when fruit is being prepared in a dehydrator.

Apples: You can flavor your apple slices by:

1. Lightly sprinkling various flavors of dry Jell-O on the apple slices.

2. Dipping the apple slices in lemon juice (1 tablespoon lemon juice to ½ cup water) and arranging the slices on trays. Then sprinkle on coconut that has been ground in a blender to a fine powder.

3. Dipping slices in a solution of corn syrup or honey.

4. Mixing 2½ pounds sugar with 5 pounds of sliced apples and letting them sit overnight. In the morning, drain, put apples onto shelves, and dehydrate. Boil

drained-off liquid to kill enzymes and use resulting liquid as a topping for hotcakes, etc.

5. Using fresh pineapple, pureed. Add orange-flavored Jell-O, mix well and apply, using a small paintbrush or spoon to apply it onto apple rings.

6. Crush raspberries and strain the juice, adding a bit of lemon juice, and painting onto apple slices or rings.

7. Sprinkling lightly with a mixture of cinnamon and sugar.

Pears:

1. Sprinkling on various dry Jell-O flavors.

2. Sprinkling with a mixture of cinnamon and sugar.

Prunes or Plums:

1. Halve prunes and remove pits; use a little bit of lemon juice on inside of prunes just to moisten. Spread this on with a little paintbrush.

2. Sprinkle with either pineapple, orange, cherry, wild cherry, or black cherry dry Jell-O.

Bananas:

1. Sprinkle slices with dry Jell-O, cornmeal, shredded coconut, etc.

Testing Fruit for Dryness

It is sometimes necessary to test whether the fruit is completely dried. The following guidelines are provided to simplify the task. (Remember to cool the piece of fruit before testing.)

All the fruit (except rhubarb, which some occasionally refer to as a fruit) should roll easily and spring back into shape without cracking. Learn to determine by the feel of the fruit whether or not it is sufficiently dry.

Storage

When the fruit is dry enough, remove trays from the dehydrator and cool the fruit thoroughly. Store immediately. Do not leave the fruit on the trays for any length of time or the product will start reabsorbing moisture and will have to be dehydrated again.

Directions for Reconstituting Dehydrated Fruits

General Rule: 1 cup dehydrated fruit + 2 cups warm water

Do not add sugar.

Let sit for a half hour or until fruit is plump. Cook over medium heat until fruit is tender and then add sugar to taste.

If you wish to use the fruit for pies, tarts, etc., cool liquid and add a thickener.

Note: If you are going to use the dehydrated fruit to make desserts calling for fresh fruit, use: 1 cup dehydrated fruit and 1 cup warm water.

Let sit until the liquid is absorbed and the fruit is plump. Refer to the Recipe Section for specific details according to the recipe used.

Chart Number 1

Condensed Directions for Dehydration of Fruits

It is not advisable to depend on any definite drying time when drying fruits. There are too many variables: the size of the load, the thickness of the slices, variations in temperature, the nature of the heat source, and the relative humidity of the air entering the dryer all are contributing factors. *Refer to the timing in this table as a general guide only.*

Product	Preparation	Average Drying Time (Hours)
Apples	Select late-maturing, firm ripe fruit; handle carefully as bruised spots must be trimmed out. Wash thoroughly and pare. Cut into slices 3/16" thick. Drop into solution (see section on preservatives) and let stand two minutes before draining thoroughly. Place on netting on shelves one layer deep and place in dehydrator.	12–15
Apricots	Select tree-ripened fruit; do not peel. Cut in halves and turn inside out or slice 3/16" thick. Drop in solution for two minutes and drain. Place treated fruit on netting on shelves, skin side down and only one layer deep, and place in dehydrator.	24–36
Bananas	Select ripe, firm fruit; trim off any bruised spots. Slice 3/16" thick and drop into solution for two minutes; drain thoroughly. Put on netting on shelves and place in dehydrator.	15–24
Berries	Use firm berries; handle carefully. Wash, sort, and drain; no other treatment is necessary. Slice strawberries 3/16" thick. Spread on netting on shelves, one layer deep, and place in dehydrator.	15–24
Cherries	Select fruit that is just ripe—must be firm. Wash and remove imperfect fruit. If pits are to be removed, take off stems. When pitted, let fruit drain for an hour (but reserve all juice as it may be bottled). Spread pitted, drained fruit on netting on shelves one layer deep and place in dehydrator. If cherries are cut in half, drying time will be shorter.	24–36

(Continued)

HEALTHY RAW FOOD COOKBOOK

Chart Number 1 (Continued)
Condensed Directions for Dehydration of Fruits

Product	Preparation	Average Drying Time (Hours)
Figs, Grapes	Wash, cut out blemishes, and cut in half. Spread fruit one layer deep, skin side down on netting on shelves and dehydrate. For best results, use Thompson Seedless grapes.	15–20
Lemon or Orange Peel	Wash orange or lemon, grate on grater with at least ¼" openings until white layer is reached, but do not grate into this layer. Place grated peel on nylon netting one layer deep and dehydrate.	12–15
Peaches	Select fully-ripe fruit that is firm enough to stand some handling. Wash the unpeeled fruit and dip fruit in boiling water for a few seconds to loosen skins, and then plunge into cold water. Remove skins, slice fruit into ³⁄₁₆" slices, and drop into solution for two minutes. Drain thoroughly and place on netting on shelves one layer deep and place in dehydrator.	15–24
Pears	Select the best-eating varieties, such as Bartlett and Kieffer. If possible, pick them before they are quite ripe; store them for a week or two but use them while they are still quite firm. Wash, pare, and core, and remove blemishes. Cut into ³⁄₁₆" slices or eighths. Drop into solution for two minutes, drain, and then place fruit on netting on trays one layer deep and place in dehydrator.	15–24
Plums, Prunes	Wash, cut in half, and take out pits. Turn inside out and dip in solution for two minutes; drain thoroughly and place on netting, skin side down, one layer deep and place shelves in dehydrator.	24–36
Rhubarb	Trim off imperfect places, ends, and tops. Wash and slice cross-wise into ³⁄₁₆" slices. Place on netting on shelves one layer deep and place into dehydrator.	12–15

Note: Acid fruits should not be placed directly on metal for dehydrating; cover metal shelves with washable nylon netting and place fruit on it. This can then be put directly into the dehydrator.

Chart Number 2
Suggested Uses for Dehydrated Fruits

(Use your own imagination for additional ideas.)										
	Dehydrated						Reconstituted			
Product	Snacks	Raisins	Cereal	Desserts	Gelatin	Tarts Pies	Cakes	Cookies Cupcakes	Bread	Fruit Leather
Apples	X		X	X	X	X	X	X		X
Apricots	X		X	X	X	X	X	X	X	X
Bananas	X		X			X	X	X	X	X
Cherries, Pie	X	X		X		X	X	X		X
Cherries, Bing	X	X	X	X		X	X	X	X	X
Grapes	X	X	X				raisins	raisins	raisins	X
Peaches	X		X	X	X	X	X	X	X	X
Pears	X		X	X		X	X			X
Peel (orange, lemon)				X	X	X	X	X	X	X
Plums	X		X	X		X	X	X	X	X
Prunes	X		X	X		X	X	X	X	X
Raspberries			X	X	X	X	X	X		X
Rhubarb				X		X	X	X		X
Strawberries	X		X	X	X	X	X	X		X

Chart Number 3
Cost-Conversion Chart: Fruit

Multiply the cost of the item per pound by the factor figure provided below. The result will be the cost of a gallon of food that you dehydrate yourself.

For example, if apricots cost $3.99 per pound, 3.99 × 11 equals a cost of $43.89 per gallon of dehydrated apricots.

ITEM	FACTOR[1,2]
APPLES	4.0
APRICOTS	11.0
BANANAS	13.0
CHERRIES, Pie	17.0
CHERRIES, Bing	17.0
PEACHES	9.5
PEARS	12.0
PLUMS	12.5
PRUNES	19.5

[1] This is only an approximate cost since there are a number of factors that can cause a small change in the figure.
[2] This figure does not include any labor or container cost.

THE RECIPES

Breakfast

Morning Sunrise

SERVES 1

Ingredients

1 beet
1 orange
1-inch piece of ginger

Beet roots contain calcium, sulfur, iron, potassium, choline, beta-carotene, and Vitamin C, as well as important cancer-fighting antioxidants. Oranges are full of Vitamin C, which will give you extra energy to start your day. Ginger is helpful for digestion.

Instructions

1. Cut the beet into large chunks.

2. Peel the orange and divide into slices.

3. Juice the beet, orange, and ginger. Stir well and enjoy!

Blueberry Flax Pancakes

MAKES 5 (5-INCH) PANCAKES

Ingredients

½ cup flax seeds, ground
1 cup flax seeds, whole
3 tablespoons coconut oil, melted
¼ cup agave nectar
½ cup water
1 cup blueberries
¼ coconut, unsweetened, dried

Instructions

1. Mix all ingredients.

2. Form mixture into pancake shapes.

3. Dehydrate at 145°F for 1 hour, flip, and then dehydrate for 30 minutes at 115°F.

Raw Strawberry Banana Crepes

MAKES 4

Crepes Ingredients

4 bananas
juice from 1 lemon
assorted berries

Cashew Vanilla "Cream" Ingredients

flesh from 2 young Thai
   coconuts (about 1½ cups)
1 cup cashews, soaked
   overnight
splash of Madagascar vanilla
1 tablespoon agave nectar
   (optional)

Crepes Instructions

Note: Be sure to start the crepes the night before you want to eat them.

1. Place bananas in food processor. Add lemon juice and process until liquid.
2. Pour into 5-inch rounds. These should only be about ⅛-inch thick, so spread the mixture if necessary.
3. Dehydrate overnight at 110°F. Do not overdry these. I start them just before I go to bed. You want them to be flexible. Begin soaking your cashews before going to bed as well.

Cashew Vanilla "Cream" Instructions

1. Place the cashews in a high-speed blender. Blend on high speed.
2. Add the coconut meat and vanilla. Process until well-blended. Refrigerate to thicken, if needed.
3. Spoon the Cashew Vanilla "Cream" into half the crepe. Top with berries and add more "cream." Fold over and experience joy!

Cacao Pecan Biscotti

MAKES 16 BISCOTTI

Ingredients

1 cup almond flour
1 cup raw oat flour
½ cup cacao powder
⅓ cup coconut butter, softened
⅓ cup agave nectar
¼ cup water, filtered
1 cup pecans, chopped

These are not-too-sweet and loaded with antioxidants and nutrients. The cacao and pecans combine to make a crisp, delicious biscotti for a coffee break or anytime of the day!

Instructions

1. Mix together almond flour, oat flour, and cacao powder.

2. Whisk together coconut butter, agave nectar, and water.

3. Stir wet ingredients into dry ingredients.

4. Pat mixture into a ½-inch thick rectangular log measuring about 5x13 inches.

5. Dehydrate at 145°F for ½ hour, reduce temperature to 116°F, and dehydrate for 3 hours.

6. Slice into ½-inch pieces. Dehydrate until dry.

Tropical Biscotti

MAKES 1 DOZEN

Ingredients

½ cup dried apricots, chopped
½ cup dried pineapple,
    chopped
1 cup ground almonds
1½ cups almond flour
1 cup dried coconut
½ cup agave nectar
½ cup currants
juice and zest from 1 large
    orange

This is a moist dough—yielding a drier, crunchy cookie—so don't be surprised if it takes longer than other breads to dehydrate.

Instructions

1. Hand chop apricots and pineapple, and set aside.

2. Separately process 1 cup almonds in food processor.

3. Add almond flour and coconut. Pulse until just combined.

4. Add agave and pulse until combined. Remove from processor and place in bowl.

5. Add orange juice and zest; combine by hand. Mix in chopped fruit and currants.

6. Form into biscotti-shaped loaves and dehydrate 8 hours.

7. Cut into ¾-inch slices, return to dehydrator, and dehydrate until very dry.

Doughnut Holes

MAKES 2 DOZEN

Doughnut Ingredients

2 cups Brazil nuts
½ cup oat flour (made from raw oats)
1 cup raw flaked oats
⅓ cup coconut oil, softened
⅓ cup maple syrup

Topping Ingredients

⅓ cup Sucanat
1½ teaspoons cinnamon

Doughnut Instructions

1. Prepare topping.

2. Process Brazil nuts in food processor until finely chopped.

3. In large mixing bowl, combine dry ingredients.

4. In separate bowl, combine wet ingredients.

5. Add dry mixture to wet and stir.

6. Form into 1-inch balls, rolling in topping to coat.

7. Set on serving platter.

Topping Instructions

1. Combine Sucanat and cinnamon and put through blender. I use a coffee grinder to break up the grainy Sucanat.

2. (OPTIONAL) You can skip step 1 and just combine the ingredients.

Appetizers

Stuffed Mushrooms

SERVES 4

Ingredients

4 cups mushrooms, divided
¼ cup olive oil
¼ cup + 2 tablespoons Nama
   Shoyu, divided
1 tablespoon agave nectar
   (optional)
1 cup pumpkin seeds, soaked
   for 3 hours and drained
1 cup sunflower seeds, soaked
   for 3 hours and drained
1 tablespoon water
1 clove garlic
1 shallot
¼ cup parsley
1 tablespoon tarragon
1 tablespoon thyme
pinch Himalayan salt
pinch pepper

Marinated Mushrooms Instructions

1. Remove the stems and gills from 2 cups of the mushrooms.

2. Combine Nama Shoyu, olive oil, and agave.

3. Place mushrooms and marinade in a bowl and coat to combine. Let sit, stirring occasionally, for at least 3 hours. I like to marinate these overnight.

Filling Instructions

1. Finely chop garlic and shallot in food processor. Place in a bowl.

2. Place 2 cups mushrooms in food processor. Pulse until they are finely chopped. Put in bowl with garlic and shallot.

3. Process sunflower seeds and pumpkin seeds in food processor until a paste consistency is achieved. Add to bowl.

4. Stir in remaining ingredients; spoon into drained, marinated mushroom tops. Sprinkle tops with more tarragon.

Pepper Poppers with Pine Nut Filling and "Bacon"

MAKES 2 DOZEN

Eggplant "Bacon" Ingredients

1 eggplant
2 tablespoons olive oil
¼ cup water
1 teaspoon smoked paprika
½ teaspoon ground chipotle peppers (I get them preground)
2 tablespoons agave nectar

Pine Nut Filling Ingredients

1½ cups pine nuts, soaked for 6+ hours and drained
½ cup cashews, soaked overnight, rinsed, and drained
juice from 1½ lemons
¼ cup water
2 tablespoons nutritional yeast
1 tablespoon smoked paprika
pinch Himalayan salt
½ red pepper

Assembly

10 cayenne peppers
Filling
Eggplant "Bacon"

Eggplant "Bacon" Instructions

1. Using a vegetable peeler or mandoline, slice the eggplant into strips about ⅛ inch thick. Set aside.

2. Mix together marinade ingredients.

3. Place eggplant in marinade, making sure all is covered, and let soak for 5–6 hours.

4. Dehydrate at 116°F for at least 12 hours, or until crisp.

Pine Nut Filling Instructions

1. Place all ingredients in food processor and process until smooth.

2. Cut peppers in half and remove seeds and white membranes. I use plastic gloves when doing this; be careful to not touch your face. Fill pepper halves with pine nut cheese and top with eggplant "bacon." Enjoy!

Spinach Veggie Quiche

SERVES 4

Crust Ingredients

1 carrot, chopped
½ shallot
1 cup pine nuts
½ cup pumpkin seeds

Spinach Cashew "Cheese" Spread

1 cup cashews, soaked
   overnight and drained
juice from 1½ lemons
¼ cup olive oil
1 shallot, chopped
1 clove garlic, chopped
½ cup sun-dried tomatoes,
   chopped
1 pinch Himalayan salt
2 handfuls of spinach,
   separated (approximately 2
   cups firmly packed)

Filling Ingredients

¾ cup Spinach Cashew
   "Cheese" Spread
1 cup cherry tomatoes, halved
1 cup pea pods, chopped into
   ½-inch pieces
½ cup sun-dried tomatoes,
   softened and chopped

Pumpkin Seed Pine Nut Crust Instructions

1. Chop carrot into 1-inch pieces and place in food processor. Process until chopped finely.

2. Add shallot and pine nuts. Pulse a few times to start to blend.

3. Add pumpkin seeds. Process until you have a formable mass, but not so much that you lose the integrity of all the seeds. I like to see chunks of them.

4. Dehydrate at 145°F for 30 minutes. Reduce heat and dehydrate 6 hours at 115°F.

Spinach Cashew "Cheese" Spread Instructions

1. Place cashews in food processor. Add lemon juice and olive oil. Process until smooth.

2. Add shallot and garlic. Process until well blended.

3. Add 1 handful of the spinach. Continue to process until spinach is well incorporated.

4. Remove the mixture from the food processor. Hand chop the remaining handful of spinach and stir spinach into the mixture. You will have more than you need for the quiche. It is great on crackers.

Filling Instructions

1. Mix together all ingredients and place in prepared quiche crust.

2. Refrigerate at least a couple of hours to set up.

Basil Sun-Dried Tomato Spread

MAKES 2+ CUPS

Ingredients

1 cup Basil Walnut-Cashew
   Spread (see below)
¼ cup sun-dried tomatoes,
   chopped

Basil Walnut-Cashew Spread

2 cups cashews, soaked for 6
   hours and drained
½ cup walnuts, soaked for 6
   hours and drained
½ cup filtered water
2 tablespoons basil oil
2 cloves garlic
1 teaspoon lemon juice
pinch Himalayan salt
pinch ground pepper

Basil Oil

2 cups packed basil
1 cup cold-pressed olive oil

Basil Oil Instructions

1. Place basil and oil in blender.

2. Blend until well combined.

3. Strain. This will keep in the refrigerator for a couple
   of weeks.

Basil Walnut-Cashew Spread Instructions

1. Place all ingedients in a food processor. Process
   until well-blended.

2. Stir sun-dried tomatoes into spread. Use as a dip,
   or a topping on crackers or veggies.

Purple Kale "Cheese" Chips

MAKES 2 CUPS

Ingredients

1 bunch purple kale
1 cup soaked sunflower seeds
Juice from 1 lemon
1 red bell pepper
2 tablespoons ume plum
    vinegar
2 tablespoons miso
2 tablespoons olive oil
2 tablespoons Global South
    Seasoning Mix (see
    page 41)

One of the world's healthiest "chips." These don't need any dips to be enjoyed. Just inhale.

Instructions

1. De-stem kale.

2. In a food processor, add other ingredients and process until creamy.

3. In a large mixing bowl, massage paste into kale leaves.

4. Place kale on teflex sheets.

5. Dehydrate at 115°F for 3 hours or until crispy.

Macadamia Nut "Cheese"

MAKES 4 CUPS

Ingredients

4 cups macadamia nuts
½ cup lemon juice
2 tablespoons nutritional yeast
1 green onion
2 teaspoons sea salt

Instructions

1. Soak the nuts for 1 hour.

2. Dice the onion, using the white and 1 or 2 inches of the green.

3. Process all ingredients in a food processor using the S-blade.

4. Spoon blobs of the mix onto teflex sheets.

5. Dehydrate at 115°F for 4 to 6 hours.

Meals

Spaghetti and "Sausage"

SERVES 1–2

Mushroom "Sausage" Ingredients

2 cups carrots, grated
2 cups portobello mushrooms, chopped fine
1 cup onion, chopped fine
¾ cup celery, diced
1 cup walnuts, soaked, drained, and ground fine while wet
½ cup pumpkin seeds, soaked, drained, and ground fine while wet
¼ cup filtered water
¼ cup Nama Shoyu
1 tablespoon Italian spices.
1 cup raw oat flour, or ¾ cup flax seeds, ground

Marinara Sauce Ingredients

2 cups sun-dried tomatoes
2 cups water
1 large clove garlic
1 teaspoon dried oregano
1 teaspoon dried basil
Himalayan salt and pepper, to taste
2 yellow zucchini, for serving pine nuts, for serving

Mushroom "Sausage" Instructions

1. Combine carrots, mushrooms, celery, and onion.
2. Stir in walnuts and pumpkin seeds, combining well.
3. Combine water and Nama Shoyu, and mix these into veggie/nut mixture.
4. Add herbs and stir well.
5. Stir in raw oat flour or ground flax seeds in batches (half at a time).
6. Shape into patties 4–5 inches across, no more than 1 inch thick. Place on screens and dehydrate at 145°F for 1 hour. Reduce heat and dehydrate at 115°F until dry, 6–8 hours. You want these to be dry.
7. Break into bite-sized pieces.

Marinara Sauce Instructions

1. Soak tomatoes in water until soft.
2. Put tomatoes, water, and the rest of the ingredients in a high-speed blender.
3. Process until smooth.

Assembly

1. Put zucchini through spiralizer. Set in colander for 20 minutes to let water drain off.
2. Top with sauce and "sausage."

Chef's Note: I topped this with grated pine nuts for a little extra flavor. I also like to warm this in the dehydrator prior to serving.

HEALTHY RAW FOOD COOKBOOK

Mushroom Walnut Veggie Burgers

MAKES 8–9

Ingredients

2 cups carrots, grated
2 cups portobello mushrooms, chopped fine
1 cup onion, chopped fine
¾ cup celery, diced
1 cup walnuts, soaked, drained, and ground fine while wet
½ cup pumpkin seeds, soaked, drained, and ground fine while wet
¼ cup water, filtered
¼ cup Nama Shoyu
1 teaspoon sage
1 teaspoon marjoram
1 teaspoon thyme
1 cup raw oat flour, or ¾ cup flax seeds, ground

Instructions

1. Combine carrots, mushrooms, celery, and onion.

2. Stir in walnuts and pumpkin seeds, combining well.

3. Combine water and Nama Shoyu; mix these into veggie/nut mixture

4. Add herbs and stir well.

5. Stir raw oat flour or ground flax seeds in batches (half at a time).

6. Shape into patties, 4–5 inches across, no more than 1 inch thick. Place on screens and dehydrate at 145°F for 1 hour. Reduce heat to 115°F and dehydrate until mostly dry, 3–4 hours. You want these to be moist, not rock hard.

Broccoli Mushroom "Stir Fry"

SERVES 2–4

Marinade Ingredients

¼ cup olive oil
2 tablespoons Nama Shoyu
1 tablespoon agave nectar or
    raw honey

"Stir Fry" Ingredients

1½ cups sliced mushrooms
1 cup broccoli, chopped
1 large parsnip
2 carrots
1 cup pea pods
sesame oil (optional)
black sesame seeds (optional)

Marinade Instructions

1. Whisk olive oil, Nama Shoyu, and agave or honey together.

"Stir Fry" Instructions

1. Place mushrooms and broccoli in marinade. Stir to coat. Set aside.

2. Peel and cut parsnip into pieces. Place in food processor and process until coarsely chopped.

3. Cut the carrots into matchstick-sized pieces.

4. Chop the pea pods into ½-inch pieces and mix into the parsnip "rice" with the carrots.

5. Stir in the entire broccoli–mushroom marinade mix. Toss. You can dress it with a little sesame oil and black sesame seeds for more flavor.

Raw "BLTs"

SERVES 2

Raw Honey Wheat Bread Ingredients

2 cups wheat berries, sprouted and ground into flour
1 cup zucchini puree
1 apple
1 tablespoon honey
1 cup ground flax seeds, ground

Avocado Butter Ingredients

2 avocados
½ cup cashews, soaked until soft
pinch Himalayan salt
pinch black pepper
pinch ground chipotle
4 pieces of bread, for serving
tomato, for serving
lettuce, for serving
Eggplant "Bacon" (see page 15)

Raw Honey Wheat Bread Instructions

1. To make flour: Soak wheat berries for 24 hours, then rinse 2 times a day until small tails sprout. Dehydrate at 116°F until dry. Grind into flour.

2. In food processor, place apple, zucchini puree, and honey. Process until a puree is achieved.

3. Mix together flour and ground flax.

4. Stir puree mixture into flour mixture.

5. Spread ¼ inch thick on nonstick dehydrator sheets. Score mixture into bread-sized squares. Dehydrate at 145°F for 45 minutes, then turn down heat and dehydrate at 115°F until tops are dry.

6. Flip over, remove nonstick sheet, and continue to dry. You want to make sure the bread dries but stays soft, so check and don't over dehydrate.

Avocado Butter Instructions

1. Place all ingredients in food processor and pulse until well blended.

Assembly

1. Layer ingredients on bread to create sandwich.

Dahl Soup

SERVES 1–2

Ingredients

1 handful string beans
1 cup coconut pulp
½ cup coconut water
1 tomato
2 tablespoons olive oil
2 teaspoons sea salt
1 clove garlic, minced
1 teaspoon cumin
1 teaspoon turmeric
¼ teaspoon cayenne pepper
¼ teaspoon coriander
¼ teaspoon kalonji
   (black seed)

This is a variant of traditional Indian cabbage dahl.

Instructions

1. Blend 2 string beans with the other ingredients in a blender until smooth.

2. Chop remaining string beans into 2–inch pieces.

3. Combine in a mixing bowl with sauce and mix thoroughly.

Mediterranean Salad

SERVES 1–2

Ingredients

large chopped pieces of tomato
large chopped pieces of
    cucumber
small chopped pieces of red
    onion
1 cup finely chopped parsley
extra-virgin olive oil drizzled
    heavily upon above
salt, pepper, and cumin to taste

This is a classic non-leafy salad.

Instructions

1. Mix and stir well. Serve chilled after leaving in refrigerator 1 hour.

Zucchini Noodles with Pesto

SERVES 1–2

Pesto Ingredients

2 cups fresh cilantro
1 cup fresh basil
1 cup walnuts
¾ cup olive oil
2 tablespoons lemon juice
2 tablespoons sage
3 garlic cloves
2 teaspoons Celtic Sea Salt
½ teaspoon cayenne pepper

Noodle Ingredients

3 zucchini
grape tomatoes, for serving

Any squash can be used—yellow, butternut. For crunchier texture, try daikon, carrot, or jicama.

Pesto Instructions

1. Process all ingredients in a food processor with S-blade until creamy.

Noodle Instructions

1. With a spiralizer, process zucchini into noodles. Mix ¾ cup pesto with noodles.

Vegetable Tempura

SERVES 1–2

Ingredients

2 cups broccoli florets
2 cups cauliflower florets
1 cup zucchini, sliced into
   disks
½ cup pistachios, unsoaked
1 cup sunflower seeds, soaked
½ cup lemon juice
3 teaspoons sea salt
½ cup olive oil
1 teaspoon coriander
2 teaspoons cumin
1 teaspoon kalonji
   (black seed)
¼ teaspoon cayenne pepper
1 cup water

"Fried" never tasted so clean! Incredibly savory!

Instructions

1. Blend nuts, lemon juice, spices, salt, and olive oil in a blender, adding water until it is smooth.

2. Combine with the vegetables in a mixing bowl and toss together with hands until all the vegetables are coated.

3. Place mixture onto teflex sheets and dehydrate at 145°F for 2 hours.

Udon "Noodle" Soup

SERVES 4

Ingredients

3 cups coconut water
1 tablespoon lemongrass, finely chopped
1 tablespoon grated ginger
1 garlic clove
5 kaffir lime leaves
1 cup coconut pulp
½ cup snow peas
½ cup red bell pepper, de-seeded and julienned
1 stalk green onion
½ tablespoon amino acids or wheat-free tamari
1 teaspoon sesame oil
½ teaspoon ume plum vinegar

Instructions

1. Chop garlic.

2. Blend coconut water, garlic, ginger, lemongrass, and lime leaves until smooth.

3. Strain through a fine mesh strainer into a bowl and discard the pulp.

4. Slice coconut pulp into thin strips the width of udon noodles, about ¼ inch.

5. Add remaining ingredients to soup.

6. Garnish servings with scallions.

Onion Bhajis

SERVES 2–4

Ingredients

1 cup sunflower seeds, soaked
1 cup walnuts, soaked
2 cups red onions
2 teaspoons paprika
¼ teaspoon cayenne pepper
2 cloves garlic
1 bunch cilantro
1 red pepper, de-seeded
1 teaspoon kalonji (black seed)
1 teaspoon cumin
3 tablespoons olive oil

Once again, there is no need for deep frying. These are a crowd-pleaser. It's hard to stop at just one.

Instructions

1. Finely chop red onions and garlic.

2. Chop red pepper and cilantro.

3. Process all ingredients except 1 cup red onions in a food processor using the S-blade.

4. In a bowl, add mixture to remaining onions.

5. Form batter into balls a bit smaller than ping-pong balls.

6. Dehydrate on teflex sheets at 135°F for 1 or 2 hours.

7. Remove teflex and continue to dehydrate on mesh for 4 to 6 hours. Balls should be a bit crispy on the outside and soft inside.

Falafel Balls

MAKES APPROXIMATELY 20 BALLS

Ingredients

2 cups sprouted chickpeas
1 cup soaked sunflower seeds
2 garlic cloves
¼ cup olive oil
1 cup leeks
juice from one lemon
2 cups cilantro
2 tablespoons Global South
   Seasoning Mix (see
   page 41)

*Sprouting chickpeas: (½ cup
dry chickpeas yields 2 cups
sprouted chickpeas)*

Soaking Instructions

1. Soak dry chickpeas in water for 12 hours.
2. Drain.
3. Rinse chickpeas 2 to 3 times daily. Give the soak water to your houseplants—they will love it!
4. Sprout chickpeas for 3 days, making sure they get air and are in the dark or semidark.
5. Before adding to food processor, boil water and pour over sprouted chickpeas. This converts the starches to complex carbohydrates.

Falafel Balls Instructions

1. Combine all ingredients in a food processor and process until well blended.
2. Process all ingredients in food processor with S-blade.
3. Roll mash into ping-pong–sized balls.
4. Place on teflex sheets in dehydrator.
5. Dehydrate at 145°F for 2 hours.
6. Remove from teflex sheets and dehydrate on mesh sheets at 145°F for 4 hours or until desired crispiness is achieved.

Global South Seasoning Mix

MAKES ½ CUP

Ingredients

2 tablespoons paprika
1 tablespoon oregano
1 tablespoon coriander
1 tablespoon sea salt
2 teaspoons cumin
1 teaspoon black pepper
1 teaspoon cayenne pepper
1 tablespoon kalonji
   (black seed)

Instructions

1. Combine all ingredients. Store in an airtight
   container until use.

Desserts

Hazelnut Chocolate Mousse

SERVES 4

Mousse Ingredients

2 avocados
½ cup hazelnut butter
1 cup hazelnut milk
¾ cup cacao powder
½ cup agave nectar

Hazelnut Butter Ingredients

2 cups hazelnuts (not soaked, dry)
2 tablespoons olive oil

Hazelnut Milk Ingredients

1 cup hazelnuts
3 cups water

Hazelnut Butter Instructions

1. Place hazelnuts and oil in food processor, blending until smooth.

2. Add a little olive oil toward the end of processing.

Hazelnut Milk Instructions

1. Place hazelnuts and water in high-speed blender. Blend very well.

2. Strain through nut milk bag or several layers of cheesecloth.

Mousse Instructions

1. Place all ingredients in food processor.

2. Process until very smooth. Refrigerate before serving.

3. Top with grated hazelnuts if desired.

Brownie Bites

MAKES 1 DOZEN

Ingredients

3 cups almond flour
1½ cups oat flour
1 cup cacao powder
¾ cup water, filtered
¾ cup coconut butter, softened
½ cup maple syrup
½ cup agave nectar

Instructions

1. Combine almond flour, oat flour, and cacao powder.

2. Whisk together water, coconut butter, maple syrup, and agave.

3. Stir together dry mixture and wet mixture.

4. Press into mini-cupcake muffin papers.

5. Dehydrate for 1 hour at 140°F, then reduce heat to 115°F and dehydrate for 8 hours.

Fruit Parfait

SERVES 4

Chocolate Ganache Ingredients

½ cup agave nectar
½ cup cacao powder
¼ cup coconut butter, softened

Vanilla "Cream" Ingredients

1 vanilla bean
2 cups cashews, soaked until soft
1 young Thai coconut, flesh and ¼ cup liquid
¾ cup coconut butter, softened
½ cup agave nectar

Fruit Ingredients

1 cup strawberries, sliced
1 cup blueberries
1 cup bananas, sliced

Chocolate Ganache Instructions

1. Whisk all ingredients together.

Vanilla "Cream" Instructions

1. Split vanilla bean and scrape out insides with tip of knife.
2. Add to all other ingredients and process in a high-speed blender until smooth.
3. You will have to be patient to get a smooth consistency. Refrigerate 2 hours.

Fruit Parfait Assembly

1. Toss fruit together.
2. Transfer fruit to individual serving glasses or plates, alternating layers of fruit, vanilla "cream," and chocolate ganache.

Ginger Peach Torte

SERVES 8–10

Cake Ingredients

3 cups almond flour
1½ cups raw oat flour
1 teaspoon cinnamon
2 teaspoons powdered ginger
¾ cup coconut butter, softened
½ cup water
½ cup agave nectar
½ cup maple syrup

Filling Ingredients

2 cups cashew vanilla "cream"
(see page 5)
4 ripe peaches, peeled, halved,
and sliced

Topping Ingredients

½ cup pecans, chopped
(optional)

Cake Instructions

1. Mix together almond flour and oat flour.

2. Stir in cinnamon and ginger.

3. In a separate bowl, whisk together coconut butter, water, agave, and maple syrup.

4. Stir wet ingredients into dry ingredients.

5. Place mixture in two 6-inch round cake pans, lined with oiled parchment.

6. Dehydrate for 1 hour at 145°F. Reduce heat to 116°F and dehydrate for 4 more hours.

7. Remove from pans and dehydrate at 116°F until almost dry.

Filling Instructions

1. Fold peaches into whipped "cream."

Assembly

1. Spread half of filling between cake layers.

2. Top with the other half of the filling.

3. Sprinkle chopped pecans on top, if desired.

Cacao Ganache Mousse Cake

SERVES 6–8

Cake Ingredients

3 cups almond flour
1½ cups oat flour
1 cup cacao powder
¾ cup water, filtered
¾ cup coconut butter, softened
½ cup maple syrup
½ cup agave nectar

Mousse Filling Ingredients

1 vanilla bean
2 cups cashews, soaked
1 young Thai coconut flesh and liquid
¾ cup coconut butter, softened
⅓ cup agave nectar
½ cup cacao powder

Chocolate Ganache

See instructions on page 47

Reminiscent of a flourless chocolate cake with a chocolate mousse filling and rich ganache frosting! The results will amaze you and your friends!

Cake Instructions

1. Oil and line three 6-inch round cake pans with parchment.
2. Combine dry ingredients: almond flour, oat flour, and cacao powder; mix well.
3. Combine wet ingredients: water, coconut butter, maple syrup, and agave.
4. Stir together until combined. Don't overmix.
5. Press cake "batter" into pans.
6. Dehydrate for 1 hour at 140°F, then reduce heat to 115°F and dehydrate for 8 hours.
7. Remove from cake pans, peel off parchment, and set aside.

Mousse Filling Instructions

1. Split the vanilla bean, scrape out the insides, and set aside.

(continued)

2. Place all ingredients in the food processor or high-speed blender and blend until very smooth and fluffy.

3. Refrigerate for at least 1 hour to firm up.

Assembly

1. Make ganache.

2. Spread refrigerated filling between 3 cake layers. You want about an inch of filling.

3. Place cake on a rack with parchment or waxed paper underneath; the wax paper will catch drips. Make sure the cake is straight.

4. Slowly pour ganache over the top of the cake. Refrigerate to set ganache.

Glazed Lemon Chia Seed Macaroons

MAKES ½ DOZEN

Cookies Ingredients

3 cups dried coconut, unsweetened
1½ cups almond flour
½ cup chia seeds
juice and zest from 1 lemon
¼ cup agave nectar
¼ cup maple syrup
¼ cup coconut butter

Lemon Glaze Ingredients

⅓ cup coconut butter
2 tablespoons agave nectar
4 tablespoons lemon juice
zest from 1 lemon

Cookies Instructions

1. Stir together dried coconut, almond flour, and chia seeds.

2. Whisk together lemon juice, lemon zest, agave, maple syrup, and coconut butter.

3. Mix wet ingredients into dry ingredients. Combine well.

4. Shape into cookies and place on dehydrator screens.

5. Dehydrate at 145°F for ½ hour, decrease heat, and dehydrate at 116°F until dry, approximately 8 hours.

6. Cool.

Lemon Glaze Instructions

1. Whisk all ingredients together.

Assembly

1. Dip tops of cookies in glaze and refrigerate to set.

Chocolate, Chocolate Chip Cookies

MAKES 2 DOZEN SMALL COOKIES

Ingredients

1 cup zucchini
⅓ cup agave nectar
½ cup coconut butter, softened
1 cup raw oat flour
½ cup cacao powder
½ teaspoon cinnamon
1½ cups raw flaked oats
½ cup chopped walnuts
    (optional)
½ cup cacao nibs (optional)

Instructions

1. Combine zucchini puree (simply puree zucchini in your food processor), agave, and coconut butter in food processor. Blend well.

2. Mix together oat flour, cacao powder, and cinnamon.

3. Stir in wet mixture. Combine well.

4. Stir in raw oats, optional walnuts, and optional cacao nibs. Mix well.

5. Press into cookie shapes and dehydrate for 30 minutes at 140°F. Reduce heat and dehydrate for 4–5 more hours at 115°F.

Lemon Raspberry Cookies

MAKES 2 DOZEN SMALL COOKIES

Cookies Ingredients

1 cup almonds
2 cups dried coconut
¼ cup coconut butter, softened
¼ cup agave nectar
¼ cup maple syrup*
1 pint fresh raspberries
*maple syrup is not raw but
    used in raw food making

Filling Ingredients

1 cup cashews, soaked until
    soft (at least 4 hours)
⅓ cup coconut butter, softened
½ cup lemon juice
zest from 2 lemons
pinch of salt
½ teaspoon vanilla extract
2 teaspoons nutritional yeast

Cookies Instructions

1. Soak almonds, remove skins, and process in food processor until finely ground.

2. Mix together with other ingredients.

3. Using a 2-inch baking ring, place the ring on the nonstick sheet, put a tablespoon of dough in the ring, and press firmly. Lift the ring, and you will have the cookie shape. Continue with remaining dough.

4. Dehydrate at 140°F for 30 minutes; reduce the dehydration temperature to 116°F. Dehydrate until dry. Halfway through dehydration process, remove cookies from nonstick sheet and move to mesh sheet so they can properly dry.

Filling Instructions & Assembly

1. Drain cashews.

2. Combine all ingredients in a high-speed blender and blend until smooth.

3. Pipe filling onto cookies and top with a raspberry.

Juices

Popeye

SERVES 1–2

Ingredients

2 cups spinach
1 apple
2 stalks celery
½ lemon
1-inch piece of ginger
1 cucumber

Spinach is good for cardiovascular health and strong bones, among other things. Apple juice provides Vitamin C and antioxidants. Celery juice has an alkalizing effect on the body and helps to fight cancer.

Green Grapefruit Delight

SERVES 1–2

Ingredients

1 grapefruit
1 apple
3 cups kale
1 cucumber
1 lime

Grapefruit juice contains lots of Vitamin C, which help prevent colds and the flu. The bioflavanoids help to halt the spread of breast cancer and to reduce water retention and leg swelling during pregnancy. Grapefruits also contain a fat-burning enzyme and help to alkalize the body and improve digestion. Apples provide Vitamin C and antioxidants, and kale fights inflammation and boosts the immune system, among many other good things.

Pear Delight

SERVES 1–2

Ingredients

2 pears
2 cucumbers
½ lemon
½ cup strawberries or
   raspberries

The pectin in pears is a type of fiber that is not lost when the fruit is juiced, making it good for colonic health. Pears also contain antioxidants that protect against brain aging. Berries are also full of antioxidants.

Tropical Punch

SERVES 1–2

Ingredients

2 mangoes, peeled
1 cup pineapple
1 cup berries, any kind

Mangoes are a good source of Vitamin C, Vitamin A, and quercetin, which helps to protect against cancer. Pineapple contains lots of Vitamin C and the enzyme bromelain, which reduces inflammation and supports digestive function. Berries are full of antioxidants.

Sweet Satisfaction

SERVES 1–2

Ingredients

½ sweet potato, peeled
2 apples
3 carrots
3 cups mixed greens

Sweet potatoes are an even richer source of Vitamin A than carrots, making this juice great for skin health. Sweet potato also contains Vitamin E, surprisingly enough. Dark leafy greens also contain Vitamin A, as well as choline and iron.

Luscious Lawn Juice

SERVES 1–2

Ingredients

1 cup wheatgrass
1 cup strawberries
3–4 dandelion leaves
    (optional)

Wheatgrass contains high concentrations of antioxidants, has anti-inflammatory properties, is excellent for detoxing, and helps to fight bacterial infections. Strawberries are high in Vitamin C, strengthening the immune system and increasing energy levels. Dandelion leaves help to detoxify the digestive track and are full of antioxidants and Vitamin A.

Skinny Green Lemonade

SERVES 1–2

Ingredients

2 apples
1 cucumber
3 cups kale
2 lemons
½ cup mint (optional)

Apples and lemons have both been shown to help promote weight loss. Kale provides more nutrition per calorie than almost any other vegetable.

Strawberry Lemonade

SERVES 1–2

Ingredients

6 lemons
2 apples
3 cups strawberries
½ cup mint (optional)
3 cups water

Important Note:

For this recipe, juice all ingredients and then stir in the water until well blended.

Lemons and strawberries are both very high in Vitamin C, providing energy and strengthening the immune system.

Youth Elixir

SERVES 1–2

Ingredients

6 leaves of cabbage
5 carrots
1-inch piece of ginger

Cabbage contains selenium, which helps to slow the aging process. The beta-carotene in carrots and cabbage will lend your skin a youthful glow. And ginger will give you an energy boost!

Energy Blast

SERVES 1–2

Ingredients

3 cucumbers
1 cup sprouts (alfalfa, clover, or broccoli)
1 bunch parsley
1-inch piece of ginger

Sprouts are full of enzymes that aid in digestion, which means your body will have more energy for everything else! They also contain the highest quality proteins, which the body can easily convert into energy. Parsley and ginger both provide an energy boost as well.

The Hydrator

SERVES 1–2

Ingredients

3 cups mixed greens
3–4 cucumbers
2 stalks celery
1 lemon
½ cup mint

All of the ingredients in this juice are known to be particularly hydrating. This is a great drink for hot days or for before a hot yoga class. If desired, add crushed ice to the juice.

Red Velvet

SERVES 1–2

Ingredients

1 beet
3 carrots
4 stalks celery
1 apple

Beets and carrots are both full of Vitamin A, which is important for vision, cell growth, and a healthy immune system. Celery helps restore electrolytes in your body, making it a good choice after a workout or for an upset stomach.

Tropical Beet

SERVES 1–2

Ingredients

1 beet
1 cucumber
1 cup pineapple chunks

Beets contain minerals that strengthen the liver and gall bladder, in addition to a number of important vitamins. Pineapples are full of Vitamin C, which strengthens the immune system.

Skin-Clearing Potion

SERVES 1–2

Ingredients

2 carrots
2 cups spinach or kale
1 apple
1 cucumber
1 stalk celery
1-inch piece of ginger

Carrots contain lots of Vitamin A, which helps maintain skin cells. Carrots, dark, leafy greens, and apples contain beta-carotene, which protects against skin damage. Cucumber contains silicon, a mineral the body uses to improve skin, nails, and hair. Ginger helps to soothe digestion, which will in turn improve skin tone.

Cold Blaster

SERVES 1–2

Ingredients

4 medium carrots
1-inch piece of ginger
1 orange
1 lemon

This juice is great to sip at room temperature when you feel a cold coming on. Carrots and citrus fruits are full of Vitamin C, which strengthens your immune system. The ginger soothes digestion and contains powerful antioxidants.

Carrot Ginger Juice

SERVES 1–2

Ingredients

6 medium carrots
1-inch piece of ginger
1 lemon, peeled

Carrots have an alkalizing effect on the blood and soothe the nervous system and digestive system. They're also rich in Vitamin A, an antioxidant that binds free radicals. Ginger aids digestion.

Carrot Pear Juice

SERVES 1–2

Ingredients

4 medium carrots
1 pear
3 stalks celery

Pears have been shown to lower the risk of developing asthma and to help prevent stomach cancer. Celery helps to restore electrolytes and may even reduce the severity of migraines.

Gentle Green Detox

SERVES 1–2

Ingredients

3 cups kale
2 apples
1 cucumber
½ lemon

All the ingredients in this juice are helpful for detoxifying your system and for weight loss. Sip the juice slowly in place of breakfast or lunch to give your digestive system a little break. If you are doing a detox for a day or more, alternate this drink with other vegetable-based juices.

Purple Punch

SERVES 1–2

Ingredients

1 beet (root and greens)
¼ cabbage head
2 cucumbers
1 cup red or green grapes
1 cup parsley

Beets and cabbage are both cancer warrior veggies. They're also good for skin health, as are cucumbers. Grapes have anti-inflammatory properties, and parsley aids digestion.

Happy Belly

SERVES 1–2

Ingredients

1 pear
1 cup parsley
2 stalks celery
1 cucumber
1-inch piece of ginger

Pears help to cleanse the colon and relieve constipation. Celery, parsley, and ginger all benefit digestion.

Standard Conversions

Metric and Imperial Conversions
(These conversions are rounded for convenience)

Ingredient	Cups/ Tablespoons/ Teaspoons	Ounces	Grams/ Milliliters
Fruit, dried	1 cup	4 ounces	120 grams
Fruits or veggies, chopped	1 cup	5 to 7 ounces	145 to 200 grams
Fruits or veggies, pureed	1 cup	8.5 ounces	245 grams
Honey, maple syrup, or corn syrup	1 tablespoon	0.75 ounce	20 grams
Liquids: cream, milk, water, or juice	1 cup	8 fluid ounces	240 milliliters
Salt	1 teaspoon	0.2 ounces	6 grams
Spices: cinnamon, cloves, ginger, or nutmeg (ground)	1 teaspoon	0.2 ounce	5 milliliters
Sugar, brown, firmly packed	1 cup	7 ounces	200 grams
Sugar, white	1 cup/ 1 tablespoon	7 ounces/0.5 ounce	200 grams/12.5 grams
Vanilla extract	1 teaspoon	0.2 ounce	4 grams

Liquids

8 fluid ounces = 1 cup = ½ pint
16 fluid ounces = 2 cups = 1 pint
32 fluid ounces = 4 cups = 1 quart
128 fluid ounces = 16 cups = 1 gallon

Index

N

Nama Shoyu
Broccoli Mushroom "Stir Fry,"
29
Mushroom Walnut Veggie
Burgers, 27
Spaghetti and "Sausage," 24
Stuffed Mushrooms, 14

O

oats
Chocolate, Chocolate Chip
Cookies, 57
Doughnut Holes, 11
Onion Bhajis, 39
orange
Cold Blaster, 78
Morning Sunrise, 3
oregano
Global South Seasoning Mix,
41
Spaghetti and "Sausage," 24

P

paprika
Global South Seasoning Mix,
41
Onion Bhajis, 39
Pepper Poppers with Pine Nut
Filling and "Bacon," 15
parsley
Energy Blast, 70
Happy Belly, 84
Mediterranean Salad, 34
Purple Punch, 84
Stuffed Mushrooms, 14
parsnip
Broccoli Mushroom "Stir Fry,"
29
peaches
Ginger Peach Torte, 49
pea pods
Broccoli Mushroom "Stir Fry,"
29
Spinach Veggie Quiche, 17
pear
Carrot Pear Juice, 81
Happy Belly, 84
Pear Delight, 65

peas, snow
Udon "Noodle" Soup, 38
pecans
Cacao Pecan Biscotti, 7
Ginger Peach Torte, 49
Pepper Poppers with Pine Nut
Filling and "Bacon," 15
pineapple
Tropical Beet, 74
Tropical Biscotti, 9
Tropical Punch, 65
pine nuts
Pepper Poppers with Pine Nut
Filling and "Bacon," 15
Spinach Veggie Quiche, 17
pistachios
Vegetable Tempura, 37
Popeye, 63
potato, sweet
Sweet Satisfaction, 66
pumpkin seeds
Mushroom Walnut Veggie
Burgers, 27
Spaghetti and "Sausage," 24
Spinach Veggie Quiche, 17
Stuffed Mushrooms, 14
Purple Kale "Cheese" Chips, 21
Purple Punch, 84

Q

quiche
Spinach Veggie Quiche, 17

R

raspberries
Lemon Raspberry Cookies, 59
Pear Delight, 65
Raw "BLTs," 31
Raw Strawberry Banana Crepes,
5
Red Velvet, 74

S

sage
Mushroom Walnut Veggie
Burgers, 27
Zucchini Noodles with Pesto,
35
salad

Mediterranean Salad, 34
sesame seeds
Broccoli Mushroom "Stir Fry,"
29
shallot
Spinach Veggie Quiche, 17
Stuffed Mushrooms, 14
Skin-Clearing Potion, 77
Skinny Green Lemonade, 69
soup
Dahl Soup, 33
Udon "Noodle" Soup, 38
Spaghetti and "Sausage," 24
spinach
Popeye, 63
Skin-Clearing Potion, 77
Spinach Veggie Quiche, 17
Spinach Veggie Quiche, 17
sprouts
Energy Blast, 70
strawberries
Fruit Parfait, 47
Luscious Lawn Juice, 66
Pear Delight, 65
Strawberry Lemonade, 69
Strawberry Lemonade, 69
Stuffed Mushrooms, 14
Sucanat
Doughnut Holes, 11
sunflower seeds
Falafel Balls, 40
Onion Bhajis, 39
Purple Kale "Cheese" Chips,
21
Stuffed Mushrooms, 14
Vegetable Tempura, 37
Sweet Satisfaction, 66

T

tamari
Udon "Noodle" Soup, 38
tarragon
Stuffed Mushrooms, 14
thyme
Mushroom Walnut Veggie
Burgers, 27
Stuffed Mushrooms, 14
tomatoes
Dahl Soup, 33
Mediterranean Salad, 34